Praise for Dan Provost:

"Dan Provost is a keen observer, jotting down his thoughts in his *little notebook,* documenting the failures of humanity, wanting nothing more than to be proven wrong. More importantly, he looks inward, exploring loneliness, depression, self-loathing, and all the truths that most people don't want to confront. He is not afraid of showing his darkest sides, which allows you to trust his narrative and empathize with his plight. I have always admired Dan's matter-a-fact style and the way that hidden in the rough landscape of his words, you find images to marvel over."

-Rebecca Schumejda, author of *Something Like Forgiveness*

Praise for Dan Provost:

"Dan Provost and I go back a long way and I've been fortunate enough to see him get to where he is now. I think he would be the first to tell you that his earlier work was deeply influenced by Charles Bukowski, and while this latest collection has a similar dark edge, I'll say this work is Provost influenced by Provost, painful, personal, the poems here no longer walk a mile in another man's shoes, but move forward to create their own path for readers to connect with."

—John Dorsey, *I Bet You Think This Song is About You* (Punk Provincial Press)

UNDER THE INFLUENCE OF NOTHINGNESS...

Poems by Dan Provost

Kung Fu Treachery Press
Rancho Cucamonga, CA

Copyright © Dan Provost, 2019
First Edition1 3 5 7 9 10 8 6 4 2
ISBN: 978-1-950380-95-4
LCCN: 2020932860

Design, edits and layout: John T. Keehan, Jr.
Cover and title page images: Jon Lee Grafton
Author photo: Laura Provost
All rights reserved. No part of this publication may be reproduced or transmitted in any form or by any means, electronic or mechanical, including photocopying, recording or by info retrieval system, without prior written permission from the author.

I would like to thank the publications where some of these poems previously appeared: *The Rye Whiskey Review, Born to Look at the Ground* (Covert Press Chapbook-Thanks Michael Grover), *Misfit Magazine, Yellow Mama, The Dope Fiend Daily, Cajun Mutt Review, Heroin Love Songs, Moran Press, Hobo Camp Review* and *Winedrunk Sidewalk*.

Thanks to my beautiful wife Laura Provost and our Bichon Frise, Bella.

I would also like to thank: My brothers and sisters—Judi and Kenny Lamarre, Chip and Jane Provost, Tim Provost and Heather Thomas-Provost, Debby Tebeau, the late Patricia Provost, my best friend John Platt and his (my second) family, Richie and Roberta Platt, Nathan Dittmer, John Dorsey, John Patrick Robbins, Scott Simmons, Steve Goldberg and Jason Ryberg for believing in these words.

TABLE OF CONTENTS

A Way of Life / 1
Never Seen / 6
A Quintet of Champions / 7
Playing Out the String / 10
Dive Bar Near the Campus / 12
Have the Balls to See it / 14
A Statement From Some Guy on the Train / 16
When I Was Part of a Sermon / 17
Overrated / 18
A Personal Storm / 19
Anniversary of Dad's Death / 20
Pop, the Television Critic / 21
Those Were the Days / 22
The Neutral Poet / 24
Lillian, the Junkie Whore Who I Used to See
   Every Day on My Way to Work / 26
The Beginnings of My Despair / 27
The Ghost of Coins / 29
To That Same Lonely Kid at Assumption College / 30
After Reading Cioran / 31
When Writers Block Wins / 33
Bloody Wrong / 35
Fake Cult Hero / 38
Former Bedroom Thing / 39
Aging / 40
Choice Words / 41
Thanks Alice in Chains / 42
Disillusioned Boy / 43
Grieve / 44

I Don't Want to Wait / 45
Piss / 47
Donna DeBonise / 48
Playing Hooky From Life / 49
Bellingham Blues / 50
Non-Population / 52
Route Less / 53
Splendidly Sightless / 55
Living on Scratch Tickets / 57
OK / 58
No Shrink's Couch for Me / 59
A Life Not in Balance / 60
To Chucky Boy / 61
The Sad Part / 63
Trailer in Conway, New Hampshire / 68
Doubled-Spaced Anger / 69
Unconditioned / 70
Poor Candy / 71
July 13, 2011 / 72
Wannabe Rebel Up in North Country / 73
Fake Insomnia / 75
Trying to Pick Up a Fat Farm Girl / 76
My Old Buddies / 77
The Wal-Mart Kid Who Wants to be Rob Zombie / 78
After a Fucking Rejection Slip (or Waa, Waa!) / 80
A Fall Season Many Years Ago / 81
Pop and Me / 85
Life Ain't Pudding / 86
The Quiet Icon / 88

Listening to the Velvet Underground / 89
A Killer's Legacy / 90
Remedial Love-In / 91
Balls of Steel / 94
The Oldies Station / 95
An Old Friend / 96
Finite / 98
Tripping on the Steps / 99
Old Henry Escorts Me off the Edge Sometimes / 100
The Green Room (a Crappy Job) / 101
The Bore / 104
Detachment / 105
Pretense / 106
Progression of Jim Harrison in the Back
 of His Book / 107
Ah, What the Hell / 109
Fucking Embarrassing / 111
No One Special / 112
Mr. Asshole / 114
Warning / 116
Way Too Late / 117
The Little Notebook / 118
The Circle / 120
The Man With the Circles Under His Eyes / 122
An Angry Phase / 125
Never a Leave It to Beaver Episode / 128
4:22 AM: Tripping on K-Pins / 129
Rampart / 132
The Vermont Car Dealership or the Jerry
 Lundegaard Hall of Fame / 134

What do you do from morning to night?
I endure myself.

—E.M. Cioran

In memory of my parents:
Arthur and Alice (Gibby) Provost

A Way of Life

Depression sucks…it's a murderer of many, the pain of existence. A lasting relationship with the knowledge that death is around the corner

That unwanted thing you never want to talk about.
The cheap lady in the goth clothes.

Your nightmare at noon
Your insomnia at 4 AM

This is what depression is
Alcoholism, flimsy drug addicts.
Spouse abuse, jobless—homeless

A shot in the heart from 10 deadly demons.
Depression? Yes, I have it.

For too many years, too many days locked up in black and blank.
Slurping through life on a bug-infested couch watching Law and Order reruns.

Crying to the shadows of dust—arranging clothes on the floor
Spare change on the table.

Magazines from last year on the desk.
CDs out of jackets.

Lost, forlorn, disgusted, angry.
Looking for one more drink to get past the plunge.

Avoiding mirrors.
Showering in dirty water
Smell, grime…a filthy sink.
Analysis of spoon-fed steps to the mailbox.
Yes, this is fucking depression. A shrill in
the daytime that no one hears

But you.
And only you.

For it's our little secret. All those who walk like prisoners
    without the key.
Bombarded with soot from a hole in your stomach.

Silent yet loud…pounding your head until your ears
    bleed into the
river of ponder.

Too tired to hear or see.

Alone time with yourself is never scripted,
only feared when the phone is the enemy and
the food on the table has gone bad.
Friends with fruit flies that comfort the pain.
Normalcy inside a spit cup. Phlegm is just
an inconvenience you cough up when there is no
answer out the window.

Plagues of ships sail in no harbor--
but inside your mind…pirates cutting your
throat with memories of being beat up by
the grade school bully.

Spitting sunflower seeds in your hair.
And you, supposedly tough guy—do
nothing but cry in the corner.

Where they know…
They know…

Cruise on whiskey highs
Marijuana highs
Light the beam for a while

Until the come down
Leading to a vial of pussy tears and
Dancing in a false pavilion.

Sickness can take the mind
Where the mind usually does not
Want to go.
But we travel there.
Oh yes, we travel there.

Until the sea and the sand and the wind and the trees and
the heartache of missing her touch.

Becomes passé and almost a basic
ritual to feed the crow again.

Man walks by and you don't care.
Fuck why do you care?

Are you a savior in this dream?
Slammed on the cross or crashed in
A building…

My spirit never could fly.

Not while my trash can is full—the men
die daily, they always do.

My actions?
Mean nothing in the sphere of things

Things that matter, then don't
But that's another argument; is this life
a choice of the living or the roll of the dice
by some goop of a being that enjoys
seeing us suffer.

A masochist wizard
        or god?

I don't know.

I never know.

So, I wake up again
contemplate the knife or the pills
or the building in downtown Worcester
that's high enough to jump off

and kill me.

Then choose neither—instead
I shower and put on a suit
of existence

Refuse to listen to music.
Drive toward fake.

Drown in my own tears
Then repeat the process the next day.

Yes, this is depression my friend or enemy.
A meddle of the mind, a shotgun
to the soul…where my contemporaries
can turn away in agony. Thanking

Their lucky stars

It's not them.

Never Seen

These things
never seen.
Want to be touched
but are whisked away
into a wind of
emptiness—A spotless
sense of road.
Frowned upon
While great forts
house the terrible and the murky.
Water flows down…so down.
Things never seen behind
old wood fences…Mother's
dresses held by clothes pins
on a warm October afternoon.
Sun drifting fast but cannot be
witnessed by those who will not understand.
These things never seen.
Thought about, felt…
But never sighed and walked away with.
A slit in the early evening…
The tooth of an old man…
Dying after a lifetime of journeys.

A Quintet of Champions

Five of us
sitting at the bar.

Day after day.
Year after year.

No one knew
each other's name

Just a glance or a token
word of acknowledgement

What's Up we
all said…

As one of us
stumbled in from the
cold.

No buttons
to push or
an axe to grind
with a soiled co-worker.

Just this gang
of nobodies.

On human maintenance
stools, searching
for discounted utopia.

Somewhere…
Nowhere…

When one rummy
breaks the silence
of the TV…

*Patience is a virtue
that is overrated.*

We all turn around
and nod towards
the philosophical nomad.

I tip my 2004
Boston Red Sox
Championship hat.

Someone says *hmm…*

Another softly pounds
his beer in cheap applause…

Others say nothing…

As I…we go back
to another hour
of pitiful stares…

A reflective moment
for the isolated mutants…
Now gone…

Lights dimmed…
Jukebox busted…
An old cigarette machine
collecting dust in the corner

Amped and stilled
…towards
a death…that
just didn't know
any better…to
avoid the Christmas rush.

Playing Out the String

Winter sun—2:00 P.M.
is death, aging,
Looking up through
arduous eyes, trying to
feed out words of
heartfelt
        something....

Surely, we have slowed
down, as we suck on that
same joint...trying to fathom
the human condition in
some renaissance, reflective
way...

Obsessing on new
portals to climb through.

Attempting to relive
the moment when it
was so cool to be disillusioned.

But the shine
        fell...

And the vision
        fell…

Then the parade ended
in a departure of broken bones…

Sealed…
Unkempt…
Unwanted…

Just another dismal failure…

Just another fade…of ideals.

Stuck within a millisecond…

Of time…

Dive Bar Near the Campus

Fifteen beers in
and you can finally
see the duck who
shot out the porch
light…

Why bother with wet
brain imagination when
you have some campus
skank sitting right next
to you—rambling on
about society and the
new voices who are
emerging in the House
of Representatives?

Ah, fuck it! You
told your wife three
hours ago, *I'm just going
out for one or two dear*

The ultimate lie…

And that duck is
still roaming around
with a firearm holstered
to its wing…

The saddle tramp sitting
next to you has fled to
higher ground…

So, give me number sixteen
bartender…Then, I can pretend
I'm Jesus Christ.

For the rest of the day.

Have the Balls to See it

Mankind hovers
while dying its hair
red…

Fitting in or
blazing out…

We have no sense of
purpose?
How lame is that!

Mankind seeks…

Seeks what…
A pajama party of
ejaculation, fetishes and
minute victories?

We are all in the same fucking boat…
I keep this to myself as I see the children
being released from school…walking
the sidewalks with their little cliques

And adolescent tragedies…

Someday this war is going to end…
Said Robert Duvall
in *Apocalypse Now.*
Damn right it is…

A Statement From Some Guy on the Train

He told me that he liked women who were amputated
    from the neck
down...no bones to pick clean after making love...
No discussions...
About anything...
Worthwhile...

When I Was Part of a Sermon

The Preacher looked
down at me from the pulpit…

Claiming *I saw him
earlier this morning, walking
with his head down…*

*Muttering to himself about
the lack of a belief in God.*

He then raised his finger,
Pointed at me and asked,
Why are you even here?

I stood up, cleared
my throat and whispered…

I don't know.

I excused myself.
Left.

And
    never
        went
            back…

Overrated

There ain't much time
left to hope for that
miracle—the idea of
the perfect her to fall
from the heavens and
rattle all your love from
the depths of something
I can't really explain…

The worship of
yourself being famous
after you're dead is
a false, hideous dream…

Immaculate anything
in your own private
walk of sub-par…

The stains of a self-
inflicted failed life
lie directly in front
of you…with no audience
to see…another item
of doubt
That
    turns out to be true…

A Personal Storm

The bullet cries and hits me somewhere.
Never mortally wounded—but I am grinning at
laughing Sam's dice…Not pure LSD, just
my own form of hallucinogenic—
I feel no pain as I sink into the
bottom of a turnkey…a safe haven
where I can bleed in peace.
A hand has come out of the
ocean and opened to me.
It has long, curved lines and
its palm has one big nail
hole to remind me that Jesus
died for something…Just don't know
what that is right now as weapons are
thrown into the bonfire…no more shooting
for today—I was hit slightly, slid down a
door onto a beach of feel…
Your storm is coming too.

Anniversary of Dad's Death

—We are struggle.
Weep on the day of
our father's death…
Look back, poor man's
passion or rich man's
values.
Put into the ground…weep again
over finality. The days of Daddy's
grins and painful spankings
are done.
Walk into the killing
fields alone.
Staggering probably—
Wonder about a
lost past for what it's
worth.
Never ending.
Daddy's gone.
Dead and buried since
2006…Ain't coming back.

Pop, the Television Critic

The first
thing I remember
seeing on Television

was Bull Conner
hosing down African-
Americans with

hoses supplied by
his bullshit of
a Police Force…

Funny, my four
year old mind didn't
understand…

Why are *those* people
being punished…

I asked my dad
and he told me…

Oh, those are
niggers son…

I never walked
the path of a
black person…

Obviously, neither did Pop…

Those Were the Days

Once obsessed
with search of
purpose with every
asshole who walked
down the street,

I've now become
the creator of old
goats' milk.

Peering out the window,
Watching the young
and decrepit struggle
to push themselves
out the door.

Since most of
all the *outlaw poets*
have taken their ball
and gone home…

There are no more
takers of having
one or ten at the
local dive, letting
out a primal scream
into the jukebox,

Play some rock and
roll that will let
me throw away
my hard-on pills…

No, I guess I've
disappeared—jogged
into the jungle and have
never been found

Or even looked for…

The Neutral Poet

*You're an errand boy...getting
a bill for grocery clerks...*Brando
once said...

Or something like that...

Because the line between truth and reality
often gets distorted...
Because you look in the mirror
and find nothing...
Because symbols along the road
just become filthy...
Because memories of being bullied
lead you to thoughts of suicide...
Because Berryman's old Henry was just a myth
Because the sadness reveals itself
by looking out the window...
Because your neighbor paints his
porch and ignores you when you say hello...
Because you forgot to use a
sufficient adjective to
describe your childhood beatings...
Because you are afraid when
you hold a knife...
Because your desire has
become numb...

Because distortion is the best way
to describe how out of touch you
are with yourself...
Because tricep indentation does
not exist anymore...
Because being the hero is
non-definitive...
Because you debate with yourself
over the reality of solipsism...
Because the cause is not
enough to fight for anymore...
Because the answers deny
the existence of questions...
Because being the classroom cheat
only brought a stupid reputation...
Because understanding is
out of business...

Because the coffin is closed...

Lillian, the Junkie Whore Who I Used to See Every Day on my Way to Work

Leader of one army, many mistaken tokens of affection.
She walks out of so many doors of false perception that it often
takes a General from the Salvation Army to point her in the
right direction.

Her followers are zombies, homo-erotica addicts, laden in the
    stale city.
Showing pussy for stumbling dwellers to reach for…
A ringing of the bell in a schoolyard. December's last day of
    school
before the Christmas break.

Her Highness is so far removed from the days of childhood;
    she wears the face
of a million physical beatings and cocaine battles.

She tries to tell—say something comprehensible.
Never.
Leading the flock into some porno alleyway.

The day has begun
for her.

The Beginnings of My Despair

Even as a kid,
I watched the clock
with direct horror…

Knowing that each
second ticking away
was never coming back…

Time, now gone—

closer to eternal darkness,

I would walk the streets with my head down…
Every day…
Consumed with these thoughts…

Didn't lead to a happy childhood.

My past,
My present…closer to death.

I would mutter to myself
sweet nothings of wanting
to accomplish more…

While my sentence of living
would continue to cloak away
towards the inevitable.
God must have not
been listening…or
maybe Nietzsche was
right…

God died a long time ago.
And was not taking
any request…especially,
From some fat, depressed boy
who feared for his life.

The Ghost of Coins

The ghost of coins
laid flat in the embers
of want…
Spinning, reeling, costing
nothing to see any
suffering here…
I play with my own devices.
Sometimes needing a nickel here,
Or a dime there to feel something
worthwhile…Not begging for a banquet
of sincerity…but a moment of truth…
Devoid of sin.

To That Same Lonely Kid at Assumption College

I wonder if he knows I wrote
a poem about him.

Advertising his loneliness with
cheap adjectives about longing.
(For anyone to talk—about anything.)

He holds black rosary beads and prays
in front of the Virgin Mary; wanting
to forgive those who laugh at him.

He is still no dedicated follower of fashion but
a wounded apostle.

Knowing God's will is sometimes hard to follow.

After Reading Cioran

No more—
No less…

Long ago,
my spirit was never pleased.

Or joyous, or *happy*.

Just defeated in living…

Awful fat man…

Me.

But is this issue too repetitive?

I do not know, it
Seems that the *issue*
is just a supervised ending…

A self-imposed prisoner…

Children born without sin…
Ugly growths that die in the corner…

Nothing to remember fondly...
Only the finish

That sadly started
in the beginning.

When Writers Block Wins

When you have lost
the ability to bleed
on the page…

To type rubbish and
kick yourself in the ass
for it…

Hope your dead body
is never found.

Your shitty poetry is shredded
and burnt…

When you have lost the
creative ability that rapes your
soul…

And spins you *further* downward.

Towards a demise where you
cannot even look at the
being that is called

Me…

When that goes,

And it looks like it has…

The world just becomes bleaker,
Existence is jaded

And the shield to defend yourself…
Is now just shrapnel…

Bloody Wrong

You want words
that *bleed?*

Feel the cuts
        on
            my
                wrist.

See the blood that
has stained my
soul for over fifty years
in hopes of ending
my existence
on this tiny habitat…

Suffer to create?
Damn right.

I did not come with
a warning from the
Surgeon General
or
from God
for that matter.

See me curl
into the fetal
position as
I strike that last
letter on the
keyboard…

You all think
you have the
right to complain…

Bitch and moan about
some society scorn

about being different?

Come live inside my
noggin for an hour…

See the sights, write
about soot, dankness…

Dark, dark abodes
that crash into shiny
deaths within every
self-involved step.

Words that Bleed?
Words that Bleed?

You don't know

anything…

about putting blood

on the page…

Fake Cult Hero

A little bit of
invincibility writing
cryptic endings dealing
with my demise…

Don't we all
want our biopic
showing us in
a contested light?

Misunderstood, exiled
to an existence that
can only be expressed
by murky poems
that convey how
my interpretation of
presence in this
filthy abode called
the world is just a
sick, sad joke…

Am I not a cult hero?

Yeah, who is shitting who?

Former Bedroom Thing

Can't be your bedroom thang for
an eight-dollar blow job that will
give you a five-dollar fix of nails and
needles—and maybe even enough
left over for a meatless taco at Pancho's.

Money's tight; even the scammers and the
low-rent cocksuckers are throwing in the
bloody red towel, crying, *we're hurting, too.*

Life never goes well for those close to
the real ringside...scabby hair blowing off
Sickle Cell harlots, dying in the junkyard, avoiding
others who pass by with lily-white smiles

Slinking *everything's great* smiles while
driving through the Main Street intersection annoyance.
Nah... I can't be your bedroom thang anymore.
I'm too poor
to attend the chapped people party.

My pockets are empty
and my emotions are full of appreciated nothings.

The seizures start at noon every day now...

Aging

Enthralled
in nothing—

Death in
mid-sentence.

We all had time
to cut the cord

As years slowly
bury us...

Always mindful

of some god-damn
lonely love...

Choice Words

There are words—never to
be said without shotgun matter
shattering the teeth with
                      untarnished blood…

Ready to be expelled from the throat
into the oblivion, masked with
realizations and rebellion…

Taken to the misguided center—where
a tar and feather punishment awaits;
along a street of forlorn dreams.

Yes, words begging to be heard, to martyr the
strange—in their journey to create…to walk in semen
infested alleys where sometimes the good do die young.

The old stags tough out and the others marvel and laugh, at
another day…
Forward…

Thanks Alice in Chains

I see…
I crave…
I feel…
Nothing…
Angst,
Manacled,
Beaten,
Disavowed, disinherited, depressed, suicidal, man in a box.

Disillusioned Boy

It was during a very early October snowstorm when I decided to drop out of the human race. I kept looking the flakes drop outside my bay window and understood: *I am not significant, nothing that happens in this life is significant.*

I wrote a note to anyone who cared that I was leaving. I did not know where or how I was going to get there—I just knew I could not play the game of existence anymore. The note emphasized that no one was to blame about this decision… only I was the one who saw no point in fooling the world that I was normal—or wanted to be normal.

Men like me are false fables. Stories invented inside our heads to soothe us through another day, week or in my case, an hour. I hated what I had become, but that was not all there was to it; I hated what everybody had become; a slew of infested rats playing in an electrified cage.

It made me sick.

So, it was time to leave…leave what?
Everything that is acted, a figment of life's imagination.
I hope the road is not taken yet…

But I never had the guts to walk it.

Not yet anyways.

Grieve

You have to
get away from the
burning hands of
some disarming fate

Leaving junkets of
disdain and distrust
from all the victims
that never leave the spirit.

We walk into a grieving
process from the womb

I guess…

Shared symbols of a
crying infant…about
ready to die to
complete the process.

I never advocated the
ritual of living and dying
to anyone…

Just take it on its
own merits…

I guess…

I Don't Want to Wait

There are no more vibes—
or salutations that
matter...

I refuse to wait
for the final bell
to ring, when I
can ignore the
Sermon from the Mount
right now.

Simple, various lies being
told in Sunday School,

heard by stunted children
who will grow up,
discard useless fables.

Become heavy, then pass
on with a celebratory band
playing Hendrix in the wrong key.

I want to ignore the obligatory
middle age...run right from
baby scar to elderly shame.

There will be no discoveries
that will *change the world.*

Only more wars, more
bullshit uttered by pathetic
people…

I wish I could bypass
all this crap…begin
my journey into darkness.

Acknowledge no-one
in this pitiful passion
play

We
Call
Life.

Piss

His wife left him
an hour ago, He
was telling me his
sad tale while we
were taking a piss in
some seedy men's room
in a dive bar…

I had a gun in my pocket,
ready to end it all…
But after talking to him…
Maybe…

Donna DeBonise

The first love of my life…
I would suck
in my fat when
she walked by with
her zit-faced best friend
Laura Stark.

I asked her out in 7th and
8th grade…

Her, being the master of
my seventh-grade erections…

Then my eighth-grade
frustrations since I
had no idea what
masturbation was.

Both times she thought
about it, then told
her pimply sidekick
to tell me
no…

I haven't been the
same since
I guess that's a bad thing.

Playing Hooky From Life

Hung around in the dive bars on the Bellingham/Blackstone town line yesterday. Saw the same stories I've seen in other places...the boozy laughter, the gossip about fights and breakups, the blank stare from guys whose only solace is a walk to the tavern and drinking shots of whiskey and rivers of beer. This is a clatter of life, a lonely life where I've blended in for years.

The only thing to do is punch yourself in the arm so you don't cry.

Old men who are almost gone, youthful drunks who are on the way to an early death, woman who are in their late 40s; it is not party time for them anymore, just another day of convenient forgetfulness. An excuse not to look in the mirror.

Oh yes, I've seen you all sitting in my corner of the dive bar world; drinking Miller Lite and noticing the laughter that hides sadness, the drunken conversation that masks loneliness, the red-eyed homeless guy that accepts finality.

I was there on a Monday afternoon...A day I should be among the working world; instead of counting the days until I have the courage to pull the trigger.

It's tough living inward among this sad, sorry cast.

But, if you really dig deep, we are all living inward here—saddled around a u-shaped confessional where, even if you say nothing—you're admitting that there is a lot wrong with you.

This is just a good place to hide for a while.

Bellingham Blues

I used to have dreams.

Now they're just warlike chants.

How long can you be anonymous in this world? Do you have to say *fuck it* to normalcy; begin to walk the streets you played on as a boy aimlessly? Talking to yourself about 1974 and Bill Lee…the extroverted thinking man's lefty for the Boston Red Sox? Just left to ponder the past, hate the present and fear the future?

Fear…that word pops up again. Anxiety—where your heart beats out of your chest when you dare go to Stop and Shop. You notice that the shoppers around you are ugly clones of existence. A nuisance of mothers screaming, children crying, and lonely old men buying a jar of microwaveable meatballs. The can collectors; smelly, grimy people who dig through garbage cans for a nickel deposit, bring bags of Coke, beer, and Red Bull. They make twenty or thirty bucks and go on to another way of survival. Head down, they look out of the corner of their eyes in shame. Unshaven, unbathed and looking for a huge tree to lie under and rest.

How do I know this…because sometimes I follow them. They wander into a park or behind the store…debate what they are going to do with their money, then rest until the next garbage collection day. Lying in the tall grass where the ticks and mosquitoes eat at their skin. Inserts of bugs sucking their blood are seen in legions up and down their arms and legs. They do not see me; I hide among the shadows just watching…

Watching them die a slow death, in the town I was raised.

All of us dying a slow death…some just fake it better.

Non-Population

To die among the weeds which are
flailing in the wind on summer's second hot day.

Body, weather beaten and decaying—no opportunity of
 conversation with the corpse.

What was his favorite book?
What were his feelings on politics?
Or a simple what's your name?

Sometimes, they find the living among the weeds also.

And nobody asks them anything either.

Route Less

Certainty…
You never had it…
Yours was an excursion filled
with ambidextrous *On the Road* episodes
and spur of the moment decisions
that led to loss of what is deemed
sturdy…

There were never any
Solids or *routines*…

Only awaking to plans
of emotional proposal and
ambiguity toward the spiral
that you thought spun out
of control when the masses
took the train, or the bus, or
drove in Chevy Blazers to
the mundane…

Certainty
You never had it…
Only you knew that
Those who chanted
My God,

Those who prayed and
Lived by the *golden rule*

Were doomed to Zoloft
inadequacies...

Erased on narcissistic looks
in the mirror and cheated on
The South Beach Diet.

Certainty,
no...
As you shared no followers, pretended
to no one...

Felt that the only certainty there is...
Is the certainty of a parallel universe which you
want to observe

Misguided to be suffered or celebrated...
Zealots to be amused by

Certainty
No...only hope
for the nothing

and a prayer for the visceral.

Splendidly Sightless

I have been on that final
cross of lost love.

Tied to a telephone pole where
twenty ancient Pharisees preached
spiritual vespers while
crows picked at my eyes…

The holy men called it convenient
blindness—as the blood dripped
off my face…

Onto the circled concrete; where one lone handmaiden
cried for my plight

I call the whole scenario a final escape;
Pardons from Eros for letting me feel too much.

Now I am splendidly sightless…The faces are dark…
I cannot see anything
               or
                   anyone.

I am a defenseless man…with no more stares
into love or desire.

Only me and the survival of one…
The one who tried to matter
but failed…

failed in the extraordinary light.

Living on Scratch Tickets

Sweating alcohol.
Living in the park.
Wearing a torn suit coat on a 90-degree day.

The lost wanderer with protruding gums stumbles to the checkout
line at the White Hen Pantry to cash in his 5-dollar scratch ticket winnings.

He thanks the non-committal clerk, picks up his coat hanger radio antenna.
I pay for my newspaper and remind myself to remember him.

Then write these words of observational suicide.

OK

It is, I guess
a fair place to
find an alliance with the dying.
The cold, dark bedroom,
sheets and linen not washed
in weeks.
Smell of must-soiled body
entrapped in walls.
Then nothing...
A silence of dawn passes through the window.
The ultimate equalizer
of end...

No Shrink's Couch for Me

All the clinicians sat around with their crumpets and attitude—the world will never change with words and Aaron T. Beck theories…A bad combination…

Whiskey and sorrow
Pain and fear
Death and Marcus Welby…

I haven't been well in years…

A Life Not in Balance

My god…when do you look at your life and run away in fear and languish? Almost 51, and Joe has no job, lives with his mom, collects SSI due to his depression and anxiety and considers killing himself every day. The sun becomes an enemy, the night a threat to your motor skills. Is this the day you finally pull the trigger… blowing grey matter all over your rebel coat? What do you do when the air begins to close in on you? Voices mean nothing; they just blend in with the blood and anguish that floats overhead. Joe is always claiming that he is near death…by his own hands. Has he mentioned this before? Has his self-serving destruction bored you?

Of course, the character Joe in this little story is not real…but individuals like him exist. They can be as close as your spouse—or the guy in the cubicle next to you; a lover, an enemy, a far-away friend—all on the verge of dying. But the great parlor game goes on, the man with all the hands moves you like little chess pieces along the board of the world. Going places we rather not go…say things we rather not say. We live in an *I don't want to* world, but we go anyway.

It makes me want to scratch my skin until it bleeds.

To Chucky Boy

Throw away the day you
were born and wonder

what a life would be
without pain or clatter

of the idiot who stands
in front of you in the checkout

line in the grocery store.

All the little mundane
episodes each must

live through as we
walk through this ugly

thing we call existence…

This pain is death Chucky
boy and dying will solve

its power…

But I have neither the strength
nor the courage to cut through tendons today…

So, I watch for new players to amuse
me into tomorrow…and hope bravery
is a trait I can fall back upon.

Because deep down I know the
cowardly lion is still out there
roaming the streets…looking
for a final victim.

The Sad Part

I.)

I wanted to die.

Looking out my window was the closest I dared myself to integrate with society. There was a cold sadness in the pit of my being. I knew I could not believe that things outside my bubble were real. Every day was that black and white pursuit—that desire to be gone from the thing called existence.

Did I have the balls to do it?

I know I digress—but it all ties into the same question, doesn't it? Having the desire to leave this thing called life and being unable to physically perform the act. Understanding that I lacked the guts to even step out the door most of the time, I realized that this might be a huh…huh…inside job where hanging, overdose on my depression pills or cutting my wrist would be realistic options to end it all.

Ha…I digress again. The times I did go out—my being was filled with anxiety, sadness and fear. I usually went to bars—hoping to get out of my mind a little by drinking and listening to music. I usually sat alone, not saying much and pouring money into the juke box listening to lyrics that I enjoyed from another lifetime ago.

Isolated among the isolated as it were…again funny, so fucking funny.

II.)   John Berryman

John Berryman once said, *Life is boring.* He was right. Damn Skippy he was right. Where do you find a sense of purpose? An attached memo within your soul claiming that you have the inevitable right to live? To exist? It wasn't my idea to be here...I wanted no process in the act of *making a living* or *observing the life around me.* I wanted to tread on a different plane—a non-secular alternative of communicating, of wanting, of companionship...I did not think these thoughts at a frantic pace, nor do I expect anything to come out of my desires...

I cannot fully explain what my desires are...

Can you...

III.)   Hatred and Being Polite

Besides going to the local pub, the few occasions I chose to mingle with anybody remotely representing society was out of necessity...but a paradox, nevertheless. Part of me wanted out—out of life, out of existence, out of anything that resembled what I was seeing outside my window. But living on depression and two-dollar crackers left me stomach to gurgle, so I would, on occasion, go to the grocery store. It was always a miserable experience...Cramped with old ladies and mothers with uncontrollable children always getting in the way. My mind was one of justified murder—you are in my way grandma; your kids are wailing in my ear mom...get the fuck away from me or I will destroy you by sheer will. But these were just thoughts, desires that I envisioned but would never act upon. I would be polite, always saying *excuse me* or grin in an accepted but haughty way. I would physically pick up my cart if the aisles were packed with gabby mothers that refused to believe they were blocking my attempt to get a frozen dinner. Putting it down...they always would look at me and mutter *oh sorry* and I would smile and tell them—*It's OK, no problem* when inside, I wanted to kick them in the tits. Their continued conversation about absolutely nothing would leave me to shudder. What if these women just melted away due to my will...my wants, my needs? But I realize this will not happen—so I do not pray to God, do not spit and slander their very existence, do not wish them any unhappiness or pain externally...I just go about my own way—grab my chicken pot pie and leave the situation completely...Aware of what is going on in my gut but not reacting or responding to any emotional outburst.

It is to weep...

IV.)   Too Much of a Pussy to Do It

I will continue to whine about suicide, but I will not commit the act. The reason, I'm afraid of what is on the other side. Living in darkness for eternity is not what I look forward to. But is this living? Who am I to say…Who am I to say anything about anything…Mothers raise babies to grow up as solid, righteous members of society, but what is society anyways? Just a bunch of programed robots who…oh, you know the question…but the answers can come cheap sometimes…They may come in a retirement plan, a drink in France, a good drunk at a dive bar—or the end of a knife. I know, deep down—I am a pussy and will not dare bring the blade to my wrist. To those who do…you have the mental stability of something that many cannot or will not comprehend. You see the worthlessness of this dice game, an understanding of the being engulfed in total sooty blackness. It is awful, it is non-forgiving and it leads to any action that will lead to escape.

God, do I hate myself…and I have said this all before…

V.)   Music

Fair alternative to being at a barbershop…

VI.)   Literature

Fair alternative to being at a funeral…

VII.)   Sex

Fair alternative to walking your dog…

VIII.) The End

I have no idea how anything ends…It is not my problem, nor is it my desire to find out…at least today. Tomorrow, I have no clue on what is up in this thing we call existence… You can only read *Notes from Underground* so many times before questioning everything becomes so blasé …Well I leave it up…to, to, to—I leave it up to nobody. The writers, politicians, ball players, musicians; all those trying to explore *it*, discuss *it*, answer *it* and decide to leave *it* all have better answers than I do…

I guess…judge *it* in your own life accordingly.

Trailer in Conway, New Hampshire

Green trailer
Stands alone…
Isolated…

No living or
dead…

Just quiet
Just failing…
Just nothing
But empty space…

Insanity comes
easy when you're the
only car on the road.

Doubled-Spaced Anger

I estimate I have about 8,200 days left on this banal planet,

Better to walk with the whispers of the hunters still haunting me—those daring accepted who wish to put a bullet into my psyche.

I will still drink and drive and smoke one-hitters while walking down Main Street USA.

Stop me—I dare you.

Pent-up emotions often leave people to hurt, to maim and to strike out at the serpent.

Good.

I want to watch someone explode radically, tell the world to fuck off and carry the work cargo off the docks and dump the remains into the water.

Join the hate race…feel the disillusionment of the hoody walkers with the hairy face and empty pockets.

For one day, one hour, join them—then go back to the rest of your 8,000 mornings of coffee and croutons.

If you want.

Unconditioned

Watching a dog
being fed scraps from
a homeless man…

You see this and cry—
Leaving the empty street
hating the human *condition*.

A vagabond on his last legs.
Only companion a feeble mutt…

Sins of nothing but
awful survival.

Poor Candy

She sits with someone new most nights.
The sniffles of cocaine mix with the hyena laughter as
I try to say something witty.

My passion for her is nil. She is a good person,
An interesting technique of poor.

But the game is always the same; whispers to bartenders
about dealers, hook-ups and woman beaters.

Tonight, she sits with Darnell and cries over a son who
has a bad heroin habit.

Darnell seems concerned—then he rubs his nose…a sign for
a chemical pick-me-up.

I turn away; smile and put a fiver in the juke box.

I'm not fooled, but I'll never
                    let
                            on.

July 13, 2011

Hardened by
loneliness
And realizing *that* woman
who would finally understand me
is not out there.
I sit alone in my office eating an orange.
Knowing at 46, I had the
same fear at 36.
Probably at 26 as well.
But I keep on going.
Trying to tell some truth to anyone who will listen.
Knowing that the way to get anywhere
is to go the path Emerson walked
and, instead of avoiding the potholes,
cherish them with honor… because in this thing we call life
you're the only one with the guts to confront them.

Wannabe Rebel Up in North Country

Tainted miracles
are just subjects
you settle for…

While waiting on
chaos theories and
lyrics by Chris Cornell
to blitz you out of your psyche.

Let go of his words trying
to become a metaphor for the
dark steps of glorified agony…

You see—Northern New Hampshire
is not a great place to walk
the strange steps of non-linear.

Cds and guns are cheap to buy
here…

And listening to Soundgarden
full blast in your car will get
death stares and unspoken
threats from the thirty-year
city veterans.

No, do not fret.

Go about your business and
keep the stash hidden…

Chris Cornell is not pictured
in the Jesus Christ pose up here…

Weed will get you ten…
Blasphemy…twenty.

In the morality jail of
the north country.

Fake Insomnia

Try to sleep
mid-morning.
Fail—

Listen to the neighbor's
circular saw cut
necessary existence;
Repairing the steps
on his porch.

I still lie in bed.
Eyes staggered…

Nearing re-birth
and re-entry…
Another centennial
of chosen solitude.

Trying to Pick up a Fat Farm Girl

After I made my smooth move
to get down her pants,
She said *I would rather
make love to a pitchfork.*

Looking back—maybe I
should have changed
my pickup strategy.

Telling an obese girl that
you would like to go home
and *swap some fat* might
not be the phrase I should have
used to help me get laid.

Unless, of course, we were going
to get really kinky.

And fuck while bathing in lard.

My Old Buddies

I am free of nothing, still
                      the fools laugh
as they linger on the street—waiting
for me to leave my apartment and wander
into the wilderness of mankind.

A hysterical chortle from beings I do not
know personally, but recognize me from chance
meetings under some needle-infested bridge.

I try to look puzzled as these vagabonds approach,
not wanting to make acquaintance with oily, musty
people who reside in the shadows.

We both know the lie I live—never conceding that my
    sunglasses
hide the mettle of a loser…a stranger inside a riddle whose
    loneliness rages
through the unspoken words.

I need to find help somewhere, a place where I can let go.

Not now however, I will walk with this cast of characters—
    inside the darkness
of days where others are like me.

We don't talk about it.
But we know
who's kidding who.

The Wal-Mart Kid Who Wants to Be Rob Zombie

Purple hair—recent High School
Graduate to the miserable
world…

The Purple Haired Kid told
me about his ADHD, how
he struggles daily to
understand what is going
on around him…

Hey sonny, you do not need
ADHD to misunderstand
what the difference is between
a truth and a lie…

He then went on about
how he wants to be a singer
once he leaves Wal-Mart.

Oh yeah, I say feigning
 half concern.

*Who are some
of your influences?*

He tells me Rob Zombie
is his idol and his son
will be *as great as him*

I nod, thank him for bagging
my groceries and leave.
Not telling him I'm a
wanna be poet circled
in a haze of detached reality.

You dream of what you
want to be I guess
Reality just caves in
the ambition…

After a Fucking Rejection Slip (or Waa, Waa!)

I have no sense
with some skinflint
dilemma of what
is right…Christ,
Your ammo-filled
words of critique
kills me when it is
deemed unacceptable
for some fellow rummy
to read…Fucking anticipate
death or real to the semblance
crowd is a shudder to
sneak a glimpse in the mirror…

You shit-heads continue
your circle-jerk somewhere
else.

A Fall Season Many Years Ago

I)
I felt like I had tiptoed through a shooting gallery these past few months…

Fighting the panther face to face.

Punch per punch…

So many times, I held
a pistol to my head…wishing
for a phone call

One.

Just one.

With a *how's it going* or
where have you been?

Tearing every moment while my hands
were shaking.

Holding that .38 snub nose I stole from my father's dresser

Saying goodbye to nobody

and everybody.

II)
Blowing off work.
Walking through the city
angered, crying…looking for
the ghost of Van Zant or Lombardi
to help get through another hour.

I *was the madness*…It seeped into
my eyes, then widened the bottomless
nothing that endured in my soul.

Each person whisking by me.

I was not there…I had already fallen.

Yes, I was still breathing…
But in reality… I was dead.

A mannequin
going through robotic motions
of existing.

III)
I would come home

Sort out half-written wills and suicide notes.

Love letters addressed to no one
thinking I was the victim

Of want?
Of unreturned endearment?
Of exhausted worship?

These are cruel beliefs for someone
who tried to be morally right.

Most of the time.

IV)
My being was a blind stare into a
catacomb of shame…
A bleeding animal, wounded beyond
a couple of scars, I wrecked cars…hit people…

Became comfortable with screams that
were never shouted…

Only in private…
Only in private…

I then sat near a living grave.
Lonely, somewhat defeated

Wishing for an ounce of prevention
but knowing a pound of the gun…

Was only a short step away.

Looking left then right; I wondered when
my final escape would happen.

When I would leave this world
and the crows filtered around my grave.

Only a memory
that would always be forgotten.

Pop and Me

Every time I go back to my hometown
I am reminded by the old locals how
much I look like my late father.
How my mannerisms, facial expressions, and demeanor
    all reflections of
a man who never ran away from a fight.
Jumped out of airplanes while serving in the 82nd Airborne.
Ran a boxing gym for 35 years—charging no fees for lessons.
Yes, I guess it is not so bad to be compared to a sometimes
    intense
sometimes subtle man…
A man of few complications and many overt emotions that
    he wore on
his Command Sergeant Major sleeve.
I look into the crystal of my own life, understand the
    complexities and agony
that are observed every day by sensitivity…
And anger…
Follow the flight of isolation to the nearest obituary of the
    living.
Letting it embrace me—with its broken crutch and heaving
    breath.
It is when I comprehend
his desire for company and a belonging to a brotherhood of
    heroes.
Compared with my hatred of society's chess match.
That we really do not have a lot in common at all.

Life Ain't Pudding

Because you have never bled with
Ray Charles on the radio
at 3 AM—after the woman
you loved told you to
get the fuck out.

Tears streaming—trouble
seeing the road...

Love and music seem
to sadly mix in the
middle of an emotional
breakdown.

You find yourself
lost in Boston, driving
through the Ted Williams
Tunnel...

Screaming at the top
of your lungs;
I didn't want it this way.

But there is no choice.

The charm of Ray's magic
fingers on the keyboard try
to keep you grounded…

But there is no hope…

You have extended yourself…

And you have lost…

The Quiet Icon

You laughed and cried as we
found the Beatles.

Because you could always
figure out if living and dying
were contained within lyrics

that seemed you could only understand.

I now kneel in front of your gravestone.

Not at all frazzled, nor sad because the
sight of you is gone.

I just wonder when the next sensational
words will be poured

all over a ground
you so proudly walked on.

Listening to the Velvet Underground

When Lou Reed cried
About all the Jim-Jims in his town.
I looked around and saw
lonely beetles being squashed
by men with no morals...

I assume he needed smack
To make him *feel something*

I guess my observation
of bugs being crushed is
pretty pathetic.

Compared to peeking
out, with a needle in
your arm...

passed out—within
a dormant dream

of nothing...

A Killer's Legacy

A river of blood and gore flows
through Jim's backyard,

as he discards all the hearts and limbs
that he carved out and off young boys
who dared to enter his den of cruelty.

Remorse? Did Gacy have remorse?
Hitler?
Stalin?
Manson?

No, no, no. Jim perceives himself as one of the lucky ones.
He views society as a wasteland of morality, a disciple of a
    diverted desire
that sees
the physical action of committing murder as a luxury that
    only few dare have.

He is a man among men.
He is a truth hauntingly revealed.

A persona of soiled mastery.

Remedial Love-In
(Donnie Trump's Southern Rock Tour 2015-2016)

Many gathered
at arenas, town halls,
Civil War battlefields.
To see the fat man with
the cheap Billy Idol haircut

They carried the Southern
Stars and Bars flags as
victorious pennants…
Waving, as the fat man
told them more lies about
how those snowflakes
wanted to take their guns away…

Dixie was playing
on the loudspeaker as
they placed their idol in
a hall of fame alongside
Bull Connor and George Wallace.

Ronnie Van Zant was blushing in his grave…

He continued to rant…raising his
chubby fist and preaching about a 1950s

America…white, Christian… *We'll*
put up with those colored people but
they ain't living in our neighborhoods…
They ain't going to our schools…
And if they get out of line…a sawed
off shotgun always will do the trick.

The Dirty South turned out for the fat man.
Many smiling, showing failed dental work.
Pick-up trucks with gun racks in the back

Rising and cheering, crying and threatening the press.
The south will rise again!
The south will rise again!
Many screamed
from Texas, Alabama, Georgia
and Mississippi…holding up
signs with many words misspelled.

They closed the Muscle Shoals studio
a few years ago. It was replaced
with Make America Great posters,
The fat man's picture on buttons,
Coins and memorabilia bricks…
Mexico is going to pay for that wall…
And please, do not mention
that guy who was in the White House
before… *He was a darkie you know,*

his wife…well, she's really a man and he
was the reason for 9-11…
He thanks them all for coming, leaving
with the crowd in a frenzy…Shouting *Lock her up,*
Lock her up.

The fat man smiled as he left the stage, his staff
whispering in his ear the propaganda he was to
spew at the next stop…

Funny, they never got around
to playing Free Bird on the stereo.

Maybe they will wait until the
tour hits Jacksonville.

Balls of Steel

Those who have the stones
to jump into the abyss
without a parachute are
self-absolved sooth-sayers.
Not knowing where they are going
to end…

Nor do they care.

The Oldies Station

To all those
70s pretty boy bands
who played that
boogity beat while leisure suit freaks were shaking
their ass to lyrics that
were written by toddlers…

To all that danced to the
fake and banal…

Fuck you.

Shadows lead nowhere except
to embarrassment and shame.

An Old Friend

He is about to die in front of me; former friend,
an important man once in my life—now, just another
guy who found this existence tasteless,
worthless…

Too strong to proceed…
Too weak to observe…

I took the knife from his
bloody hand, wrist bleeding,
stomach drenched in final pursuit.

He was trying to say something—

Worth, worthless? I
 couldn't make it out.

Staring at the blade
Wondering if I should
put it to my wrist.

Scared?
Sacred?
Faceless?

I stare at my demise a lot
these days—

One step.
One dead friend
at a time.

Finite

I do not find any landscape beautiful, nor do I look forward to vacations or escapes from reality. All is finite—it will end with the mountains crumbling, or the week in paradise ending. Everything we touch, feel, gives us pleasure will be gone.

Our life is just a race to the finish. In between are experiences, thoughts and pleasures that help us take our mind off the final, the inevitable, the conclusion; we will all die and become no more.

I detest thinking this way—but it is the truth. The gun, sickness, the knife, the road accident all fall under the heading of end. This is a fearful thought... (for me anyways) but lying in the grave or being burnt into ashes when our number is up is just the flow of evolution.

Life, love, happiness is just a stopgap, ignoring what will happen eventually.

Jimi: And so, castles made of sand...slip into the sea, eventually.

I don't want to feel anymore. It is too tiresome, too cumbersome on the mind. Feeling leaves

States of mire inside me. Goo and Gup that add to the emptiness I already am experiencing.

I fucking hate it...I detest it...
Go the hell away...

Tripping on the Steps

We walk up
and down the
steps…each day,
many each hour…

Many each minute…
Accomplishing nothing…

But putting the key
into the lock,
To an empty space…
Cluttered with
Limbs…
Hearts…
Manifestos…

Seen by no one.

Lacking the will,
The spirit…

The nerve—

To facilitate the
Process…

On deciding

anything.

Old Henry Escorts Me off the Edge Sometimes

Promises the Dream Song dared to make
were trying to hinder my appetite for
immature closure—dire steps were
needed to be taken as I endured
another season of debating whether
to leave the house.

My wife is very patient with me.
Helps me to care for my own devices.

Takes into consideration that Henry would
convince me to put a fiver in the juke to
play some David Gilmour and the rest of the
squad.

She knows Henry is some sort of distorted
creep, but, bless her heart, puts up with him.

I guess, some days he keeps me alive...

Persuades me that penance is only
for the asking...

Not the taking of

some cheap romance tale
of sympathy.

The Green Room (A Crappy Job)

Ja'Quell was a Crip.
Threatened to cut my balls off…

Those gangsters
kept coming…

Needing to be removed
from class day after day…

Stevie was a Satan worshipper.
Said he had something for me
next week…

Still, the demons
kept coming…

Fighting in the
isolation room with
some sixteen-year-old

Who had a no-show
father, a crackhead
mother…

Some psychotic
would spit at
me…

Yelling that he would
kill my parents…

But those troubled kept on coming…

Or I would have to get them.
Tipping over desks, having
books, pens and any
piece of school shrapnel
thrown at me.

Jamie was a tough
homosexual…He would
get mad if someone made
a play for some kid he liked…

And they kept coming…

Having to hold the door shut with
my foot while Chi-Chi had
a breakdown.

Would have to restrain him
so he wouldn't
hurt himself…

Or me…

They always kept coming to
the Green Room…Teachers
and staff would run in terror…

But the behaviorally challenged kids
always came to the
Green Room…

Eight hours a day…
Until I could leave and
go home…

Then start the whole
thing over again
the next day…

The Bore

The same melting
of style

Movie is getting
        boring…

I dampen the usual
ideas of suffering…

Accomplishing very little
in the frail, weak triumph
of putting on my pants.

Agoraphobia, sounds
like some transmitted disease.

Acquired from eating
too many spiders.

Crying alone is so tedious.

A work in progress

no more.

Pulling the trigger now
seems much too late.

Detachment

So, what happened to you?
Always the question
for those who think
      you're crazy…

Some days are just filled
with limited space.

Pretense

Ego fascinates the dull.
Experience the rise
of nonsense.

Progression of Jim Harrison in the Back of His Book

—Young Man:
Simple, unwavering…not knowing if he would soon
                be stepping into the shoes of an icon…

Words deliberate—maybe, unintentional?
But just—thought provoking to
a reader who envies essence,
but cannot see the options
                that surround him.

—Middle Age:
Lived, saturated with nature and
nurture of life's sacred secrets…

his search for genuine is
heroic…loyalty to his
friends and animals are
                morally
                unique…

realizes he is phasing into another mortal plane…
Worships, mourns…love and hate.

—Old Man
Ending, prepared for the final
                                reel.

But he has walked the steps of
necessary observation.

No boasting of
                trials won or battles
                              lost.

The jaunts through the land are
aged with finality.

He knows…

He will connect with the
murdered bear.

The suicide of Yesemin…
His young niece…

Somewhere/nowhere…joining the dead plant…
The dead gods…the dead birds.

Who served Jim so well,
Drunkenly violent and humane.
In his duality of
                time and space.

Ah, What the Hell

When he finally exposed
his philosophy on writing,
Jack Smithson told those
who cared, that
writing was just for the hell of it...

*Take out of my poetry
whatever you want...*
He claimed, sipping a
beer...

*If you like it great, if
not—that's fine too.*

Jack didn't last
long in this world...

He fell along
the side of the road...

Fading into a bleak
pile of stones. He

stood in the entrance of a
temple for a while...

But realized that so many
assholes considered themselves

poets… he
had to get away from
content expression…

So, Jack still lives
in an unmarked grave…

Looking out the
window…

Observes his choices…

Stains the rug
with feeling and
tossed syllables
occasionally…

Lauds spellcheck.

Then goes back to
bed—understanding
that leaving the
keyboard without
any spilled blood
is nothing
but forced typing…

Fucking Embarrassing

Shame—discourse
degradation,
—the sorrowful moment…
Letters and scripts
incarcerated in
debauch…
My prize/a mercy killing…

No One Special

These crow feet and
squint badges have seen
a lot in 57 years of existence.

Witnessed uniformed terror and
earned courageous medals for
scrapping versus a living hell.

Walked into a fire of hate daily…

Saw the ending of an earth—and
cheered.

Did this all without leaving the ground.

Or the city.

Just jammed my way through everyday shit
mumbling to myself.

About my fit into this location.

Swore it would be the last time

A million times.

Then do it again

with hazel eyes.

Mourn the love
that I always lost
in the end.

Due to me
and only me.

Confessional write?
You bet.

I don't care to judge
what is always in front of me.
So I walk away…like I always do

Confession of delirium.
Whispers from God
to leave.

Mr. Asshole

It's a great
justification for
all those who suffer
from depression and anxiety
that "getting out of your head"
is the reason you, sometimes,
drink twenty Miller Lites.

Smoke ten pipe hits of the weed.

And take credence that the
world is all right for a while.

No, not really…

The truth is that asshole has crept
into your life again.

Not as often

Not every day…

But he still lingers around the
Periphery. Peeking, hiding—
Welcoming back the guilty
hangover,
when, while groaning in bed…

All you want to do is swallow
the bullet—Cursing your existence.

No, I do not make
the cut anymore…

Walking around dazed.

Pondering creative ability
under the influence.

When you have difficulty
picking up the pen…

Yes, I hate that asshole
who has hounded
my footsteps for so many
God damn years.

He laughs when I'm
fucked up…grins

when I make a fool of
myself…

Calls me out when
I try to stay sober.

Kills me if
he wins…

Warning

I'm drunk.
I'm a bad motherfucker with
a distaste for the world.

So—a warning?
Heed my advice and run
away.

Before my kind survives
and drinks some more.

Way Too Late

And at all the
high points
of craziness…

Huey, Selby,
Kaufman

All the assholes
who spurned their
chance at normalcy…

With a thimble
      parade

of one…

Preaching to the silhouette
choir…
    Following.
Not following

mirth in the end.

Candidates that
      sparkled
      then
      faded…

The Little Notebook

I carry my little notebook to the park;
jotting simple observations…

Just to prove I can witness…

To guess people
        wrong…

Making mistakes about him or her is
the most humane event in our psyche…

It brings us down to the level of tragic hedonism.
Twisted, and puckered out of
forgotten kisses and
stares…

Yes, yes…I carry this little notebook
in my pocket to understand failure…

To accept, but more
importantly to see all the
budding traps an occasional
man or woman may fall into.

Stable territory in my quiet corridor,
while hoping someday to return
to a place where once, my name was known
and my failures are
                accepted.

The Circle

What can it be?

She hears laughter in the distance.

Maybe now taking hold of his hand
will succeed.

Her circumference abode is
not camouflaged but aware.

Of Mr. Rabbit blanketed through the
deep snow.

Of the crow who caws for
the one spectacle that inhabits the
circle with her…

A lone worm; dead and frozen,
hunted for the warmth of the hunter.

He enters, holding his soul…
For that one chance to place himself
within her.

But…
But…

She is on a journey of enlightenment…a
redemption worthy of Sun Ra and Apollo
to verbalize in legend and song.

There is no room for him within
the sphere of her crystallized domain.

She will sail with a discovered radiance…
He will pocket his losses and go…

Away from her rings of chancel beauty…
Because no altar of illumination can comfort
chances that never existed.

The Man with the Circles Under His Eyes

Foreign rain falls and splashes the headstones of
the neighborhood graveyard.

While thirty feet away, children are under red
umbrellas, skipping their way to finger-painting
class.

The man with the circles under his eyes stands
under a deli canopy and waits…and waits,
watching the act in front of him—he himself
once was a skipper, now he feels the storm
splattered upon his face.

He leaves the safety of the of the sandwich shelter and
walks to the cemetery, leaning on a statue of the
Son of God.

He observes Jesus' face staring down at him, tears
From the rainstorm streaming down the Lord's face…

Getting the man with the circles under his eyes' faded
hat all wet.

As he continues to stare at the monument of
good, he hears a voice, a whisper at first—but
seems to get louder and louder in his head…

Repent and Rejoice.
Repent and Rejoice.

The man with the circles under his eyes looks around the cemetery. He sees a woman crying, grieving the loss of her baby.

He sees an elderly couple place a flag at a tomb of their son, a known soldier who died looking for weapons of mass destruction.

The man with the circle under his eyes walks further—away from the statue, but the voice remains in his mind:

Repent and Rejoice.
Repent and Rejoice.

He again examines the graveyard, silently muttering to himself,

I repent for nothing, I'll rejoice when mankind glances in the mirror and sees...sees...sees.
The man with the circle under his eyes does not finish his comment...

Putting his hand in his pockets...

He pulls out a gun…

The man with the circles under his eyes falls down…

He never looks back.

An Angry Phase

Goodbye all you punks
Stay young and stay high
Hand me my checkbook
As I crawl off to die…
　　　　　　"They're All in Love"—The Who

To all you pandering
little poets out there
who plead for love, peace
and hugs.

Life is a fucking war.
Where many times, the
asshole in the room wins.

While you read all your
pretentious shit to the polite
yet bored crowds—applauding
graciously after you describe
some earth-shaking example
about the bowel movements
of Baby Junior, or detail the
sleek mountains that provide
inspiration to the flower power
mind.

I am fighting the urge to stand
up, approach the podium—and
punch you in the face.

Square, right in the jaw—then
take a shot at your ubiquitous
nose…that, frankly, takes
up half the room and all the
attention of the well-read but
stuck-up audience who never uttered
a swear word in their life.

You're not helping matters with
all your pussy bullshit.

And, if you bring politics into the
equation…you are telling me something
I already know…

Trump is not just an asshole, he is a
mindless fruit loop who also needs a
punch in the face for the sake of human
decency.

I might piss off some of the so-called
writers out there—but I really don't
care.

I'm tired of the fake appreciation, the
banal *I'm so disillusioned I drink and
cry* rhetoric that I read and hear today.

I'm going back to who I was...

Speak nothing...
A constant growl on my face...

Ready at the wheel...

To attack, harm and fistfight...
All the posers out there...

Who think they are real *Poetic Outlaws.*

Never a Leave It to Beaver Episode

She was a face from a 50s
                          Pulp magazine.
Cool for sleaze.
Comfort for boys who needed an outlet for
                                    busty
worship.

Lipstick too red.
Dress too tight.
A harlot in distress for libido.

Cigarette, inhaled tits heaved then
expanded…a cloud of billowy smoke
surrounds her devilish charm.

Haze of sultry between streams of tobacco.

Ultra-vixen that Wally or the Beav never
mentioned to Dad on the car ride to Friends Lake.

Dames like her were strictly beat-off propriety.
Photos hidden under feared mattresses.

Hoping never to be found by Hugh Beaumount.

4:22 AM: Tripping on K-Pins

23 Klonopin and a case of beer;
Still, I talked the doctors into letting
me go home.

Five hours later, I was roaming the streets;
Looking for a new minotaur to battle.

I Am a Bull-God.

Sorry Kid Rock.

You thought of the song—but I
was the inspiration.

Not even trying to kill myself
can stop destination anywhere.

I defied death, went to the abyss…
In my sleeveless shirt.
With no tattoos.
With no Samaritans of mercy to sing to me.

Just an idea…a journey into
Arthur's *Season in Hell*…

I played sly tricks on madness too, Rimbaud.
But refused to say uncle when the
fire got too hot.

Motifs are never simple when the
rain and the wind last seven days
And thirty-two nights.

Staggering for a thought…
Apoplectic lethargy while
tripping through Worcester
via one-way Main Street
(Why do I think such thoughts?)

Knocking on bricks towards eternal love that
pangs when I move the slightest degree to the
left—because I want to be so good in spirit but
the combustible aftershock of a pleasant duration always
leads me back to the mire.

I'm sick of waiting in the muck alone.
Tired of crisis and despair—a wanton creature
of forced defiance.

A slave of misdeeds I thought were true, just a
minute in the sphere of existence.

We are all that (stuck); despite what she thinks, or
he thinks or I think.

Games are for fools who never get to live twice.

Only one chance at the precious.

Never two opportunities
Only one…
One time…
    For clarity.

Rampart

A cast of characters
talking, lying—
Cheating on their taxes...

Their wives...

Spewing more
Kafka vomit to endorse
aptitude among the
assholes who need intellectual
justification.

Journey far from
those who keep pushing
the form rather than the
meat.

The air is thick
up there; poets,
generals, novelists,
stockbrokers...

Senators...

Will all try to block
us in with
runaround rhetoric.

Sample if you must,
but take it as a grain
of shit. Move on,
carry your story, your
sights on what is in
front of you.

This trip don't last long
friend, enemy or whatever
the hell you are.

Let the sellers sell…
The talkers ramble…

In time—everything ends.

No need to fret…*they,* us—

Me.

Have no control over sealed

fate.

The Vermont Car Dealership or the Jerry Lundegaard Hall of Fame

Narrator: Stoic Observer

Kissing the Cows, explains
one rustic gummy to another

Hiding her chocolate teeth as
the lunkhead salesman, dressed
in tight polo shirt—flexes another
bicep pose to flushed granny...

The giddy receptionist blushes
watching Joey Stud.

Dreaming of a four o'clock
rendezvous with flowers
and condoms.

The mechanics watch
in disdain...secretly
hating the sales whores
for their obviousness of
sluttish character

*They'll do anything
for a buck*, one gearhead
whispers to another.

Adjusting his Pennzoil
greased hat…wiping his
oiled hands on filthy overalls…

Shaking his head while realizing
he has to converse with these money
scumbags about repairs…

A brainy customer, reading
Steinbeck—conversing on
the telephone about his
son's loss of mortal soul…

Loud enough to hear throughout
the facility, heads snap to attention
and stare…

All slightly embarrassed and
Stigmatized at the same time.

The gerrymandering in the
Manager's office…big guy
with ponytail and ironed
khakis making his case
for a deal…

Boss man frowns, grins
taps fingers on desk…

Negotiate, devoid of
morals... *Let's not
cut too much,* baldy authority tells
his minion.

Overworked and overwhelmed
mother crawls in with infant in tow
and a two-year-old attached to
her hip...

Junior is screaming at the
top of his lungs while Mama
fights to keep some sanity
within the situation, picks
the kid up and kisses his cheek...

The soothing fails, he begins to
wail again...

There is no joy in
witnessing this crap,
Mr. Observer acknowledges
to himself

A microcosm of
uninterrupted
scripted
bullshit....

A prime example of
those who pride
themselves as pariahs
of necessary evil…

Gains by a cheap
dog-and-pony show.

That is rehearsed every day
without the victim's knowledge.

Sign here, consider this warranty.
Yeah, but that trucoat …

Somewhere, Jerry Lundergaard
laughs…

With the devil in
car salesman

hell…

Dan Provost's poetry has been published throughout the small press for a number of years. His work has been nominated for the "Best of the Web" and still loves football and music. He lives in Berlin, New Hampshire with his wife Laura and their dog, Bella.

www.ingramcontent.com/pod-product-compliance
Lightning Source LLC
Chambersburg PA
CBHW030331100526
44592CB00010B/658